T0197573

Long Haired Hippie Boy

Nashell Schwartz

Copyright © 2020 by Nashell Schwartz. 811161

All rights reserved. No part of this book may be reproduced
or transmitted in any form or by any means, electronic
or mechanical, including photocopying, recording, or by
any information storage and retrieval system, without
permission in writing from the copyright owner.

To order additional copies of this book, contact:
Xlibris
1-888-795-4274
www.Xlibris.com
Orders@Xlibris.com

ISBN: Softcover   978-1-7960-9511-1
        Hardcover   978-1-7960-9512-8
        EBook   978-1-7960-9510-4

Library of Congress Control Number: 2020905421

Print information available on the last page

Rev. date: 03/23/2020

Dedicated to my kids, Aspen, Logan, Nathan, Zachary, Hayden, and Emerson. Without all of you I wouldn't have these stories.

I have messy hair, I just woke up.

"Mom can you brush my hair?"

Somedays I like my hair up,
somedays I like my hair down.

I like when mommy puts my hair up,
so it's not in my face.

I love to play football with my brothers.

I wear a hat at the park,
it helps keep the sun off my face.

I like to have picnics with my friends.

"Look he has long hair too!"

It's so much fun to play cars with my brother. "Vroom, Vroom"

Playing dress up is soooo much fun...

I can be a dragon, or a lion, or a pirate or, or, or... "dad can you be a knight?"

Who doesn't love to stomp in the mud?

My hair is long and I wear a necklace.

That's me, a long haired Hippie Boy.

Come swing with me.

Printed in the United States
By Bookmasters